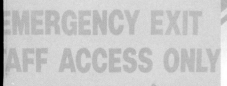

Loyal She Began, Loyal She Remains.

ONTARIO

Population: 13,792,052

Population % of Canada: 38.5

Land area: 917,741 square kilometres

Freshwater area: 158,654 square kilometres

Total area: 1,076,395 square kilometres,
Canada's second-largest province

Capital of Ontario: Toronto (pop: 4,000,000 app.),
Canada's largest city

Captial of Canada: Ottawa (pop: 870,250 app.)

Time Zones: Mostly Eastern Standard Time Zone.
Some of Western/Northern Ontario is in the
Central Time Zone.

Official Flag: the Red Ensign

Coat of Arms of Ontario: a green shield with three
golden maple leaves surmounted by the Banner
of St. George, a red cross on a silver background.
The Latin motto is translated as "Loyal She Began,
Loyal She Remains."

Official Flower: Trillium

Official Gem: Amethyst

Official Tree: The Eastern White Pine

Official Bird: The Common Loon

Top International Import Supplier: United States

Top Five International Export Market: United States

Precipitation, Northern Ontario: varies from
70-97 cm per year

Precipitation, Southwestern Ontario: averages
about 95 cm per year

Temperatures:
Spring: March to May, from 8° to 18°C
Summer: June to mid-September, from 21° to 31°C
Fall: Mid-September to November, from 7° to 17°C
Winter: December to February, from -4° to -18°C

greenwin.ca   verdiroc.com

COVER

Space may be at a premium, but those who have found their
paradise here make the most of it.

THE THOUSAND ISLANDS

PREVIOUS PAGE

Lucent rays break through the trees where the Amable du Fond
River tumbles into Smith Lake from Eau Claire Gorge Falls.

CALVIN

Design and captions by Catharine Barker, National Graphics, Toronto, ON Canada

Copy Editor: E. Lisa Moses

Nimbus Publishing Limited
PO Box 9166, Halifax, NS Canada B3K 5MB
Tel.: 902 455-4286

Printed in China

Library and Archives Canada Cataloguing in Publication

Fischer, George, 1954-, author

    Ontario moments / George Fischer.

ISBN 978-1-77108-437-6 (hardback)

    1. Ontario--Pictorial works. I. Title.

FC3062.F57 2016   971.30022'2   C2016-904343-6

Ontario
MOMENTS

PHOTOGRAPHY
GEORGE FISCHER

NIMBUS
PUBLISHING

nimbus.ca

Moments
with
friends
are never
wasted
time.

—George Fischer

To my good friends at Verdiroc/Greenwin, especially Cary and Ronda Green:
Thank you for your support.

A golden sky tints the waters near Sugar Island.

GEORGIAN BAY

Foreword

As my home for 30 years, Ontario is such an integral part of who I am that pieces of it always go with me, no matter where in the world I travel.

My passion for this huge, diverse province pushes me to explore deeper and deeper into its treasures. I roam from Canada's southernmost point near Pelee to the Manitoba–Ontario border and Hudson Bay in the west and north, then east to the St. Lawrence River. And with 17 percent of its one million square kilometres covered by lakes, the province is aptly named "Ontario" from the Huron word for "beautiful water."

Ontario has also produced some of the world's most talented and celebrated artists, journalists, athletes and scientists. So as a landscape photographer and outdoorsman, I like to think I am in good company. While my home is in Toronto, I have some favourite getaways to the near north. At my country house in Simcoe County, I plan for summer weekends with friends at the local community tennis courts so I can squeeze in a few more games. I always look forward to our annual men's weekend on Georgian Bay's Sugar Island where BBQ is the order of the day. I can drive, of course, but give me a bike and some extra time and I'll opt for cycling excursions. These can go to my cottage from Toronto or around the Thousand Islands Region. And in winter, you can find my cross-county ski tracks around Orillia, Muskoka and Haliburton.

Because the province is so vast (30 percent larger than the famously huge U.S. state of Texas) and my wanderings take me so far and wide, I have clustered my experiences randomly around five themes that reflect the most precious "moments" from my viewpoint:
- time
- culture
- nature
- art
- trade.

Ontario has left an indelible imprint on my soul. This book is a journey of love and joy for one of the world's most enduring and fascinating places. I hope you will find my emotions contagious.

Richly coloured autumn leaves against an intense
blue sky are harbingers of winter.

NEAR BRECHIN

Tews Falls, the highest waterfall in southern Ontario
other than Niagara, spills delicately over a spectacular
enclave of the Niagara escarpment.

HAMILTON

PREVIOUS PAGES
Built in 1881, the West Montrose Covered Bridge is
also known as "The Kissing Bridge."

WEST MONTROSE

Upper Canada Village brings moments of the 1860s
to life. Costumed guides explain the social life, music,
religion and politics of the day.

MORRISBURG

Sit back on the chesterfield, kick off the
runners and enjoy a double-double while
learning about Ontario. Sorry I wasn't able
to photograph every town eh, but the book
would've been a lot bigger!

—George Fischer

moments in time

When I paddle the peaceful rivers of Muskoka, Haliburton and Algonquin in my canoe – or sometimes run the rapids – I feel a connection to the Aboriginal peoples who arrived in Ontario 10,000 years ago, conquering the waters in birchbark canoes.

I also enjoy tracing the routes of the province's first European explorers – the legendary French-Canadian "voyageurs" – who left us with a legacy of song, imagery and folklore. During the 17th and 18th centuries, they loaded up enormous canoes with beaver, lynx and otter pelts they purchased from the natives to sell to Europe's elite. The lucrative fur trade soon attracted the English to the area as well, while wars with the Americans eventually drove increasing numbers of British Loyalists northward. In 1668, Hudson's Bay Company – Canada's oldest retailer – established operations at the mouth of the Rupert River to serve English traders.

Modern explorers like me can canoe through provincial parks or wilderness, visit the Canadian Canoe Museum in Peterborough, relive the fur-trading era at Fort William Historical Park and buy a genuine Hudson's Bay point blanket at any Bay store.

Fortunately for history buffs, the province is also dotted with pioneer villages, stone forts, historical castles and landmarks where we can walk in the footsteps of citizens past. Among those were heroines such as Laura Secord, British allies such as Mohawk war chief Joseph Brant, and abolitionists such as Rev. Josiah Henson, immortalized in Harriet Beecher Stowe's novel, *Uncle Tom's Cabin*. Parts of Ontario such as Niagara-on-the-Lake, Ignace and Camp Picton are said to be haunted, so visitors may even encounter some wandering spirits.

History continues to be made in Ontario as we host international sports events, give birth to world-class talent and welcome new Canadians from around the globe.

Ford's Model A followed the Model T. Its top speed was roughly 105 km/h.

A Mennonite farmer exits West Montrose Covered Bridge in his buggy. Since the rushing water below could frighten horses, the bridge's walls help buffer the noise.

The energy of 168,000 cubic metres of water pouring over the Canadian Horseshoe Falls thrills visitors from America onboard the former *Maid of the Mist*.

NIAGARA FALLS

Covered by one–fifth of the world's fresh water, Ontario contains more than 250,000 lakes. Add rivers and streams to the equation and you'll find a paradise for fishing.

Morning mist billows over the cool St. Lawrence River, the most important commercial waterway in Canada.

BROCKVILLE

A common sight in Ontario's winter months, soft mounds of snow create a white landscape of light and shadow.

Stretching across 20 kilometres, the world's largest freshwater sand barrier provides an idyllic summer beach. Sandbanks Provincial Park is the place to smell the wildflowers and enjoy a slice of nature.

PICTON

Tree branches drenched by chilly waves and frozen by cold air are weighed down by long icicles.

NEAR LAGOON CITY

Sunset across the water creates a stark silhouette. Numerous communities surround the lake.

LAKE SIMCOE

Clear, turquoise waters lap the shores of Cabot Head
Provincial Nature Reserve. The northern portion of the
reserve is within the Bruce Peninsula National Park.

MILLER LAKE

Thick marshland outlines the rich natural habitat in Halstead's Bay. River marshes are exceptional places for spotting wildlife such as marsh birds, beaver and muskrat.

NEAR IVY LEA

World-famous as an important birdwatching site and monarch butterfly migration area, Canada's southernmost point on the mainland sees many species not found anywhere else in the country.

POINT PELEE

Pine branches are encased by an icy glaze during a surprise ice storm.

TORONTO

A windswept pine clings to the Canadian Shield, known for vegetation that can handle long cold winters and short hot summers.

SUGAR ISLAND, GEORGIAN BAY

Summer recreation beckons at the Cape Hurd
Channel where the waters of Lake Huron meet
Georgian Bay.

NEAR TOBERMORY

Paddlers flock to a deep-water swimming dock off the
sandy shores of Joel Stone Park.

GANANOQUE

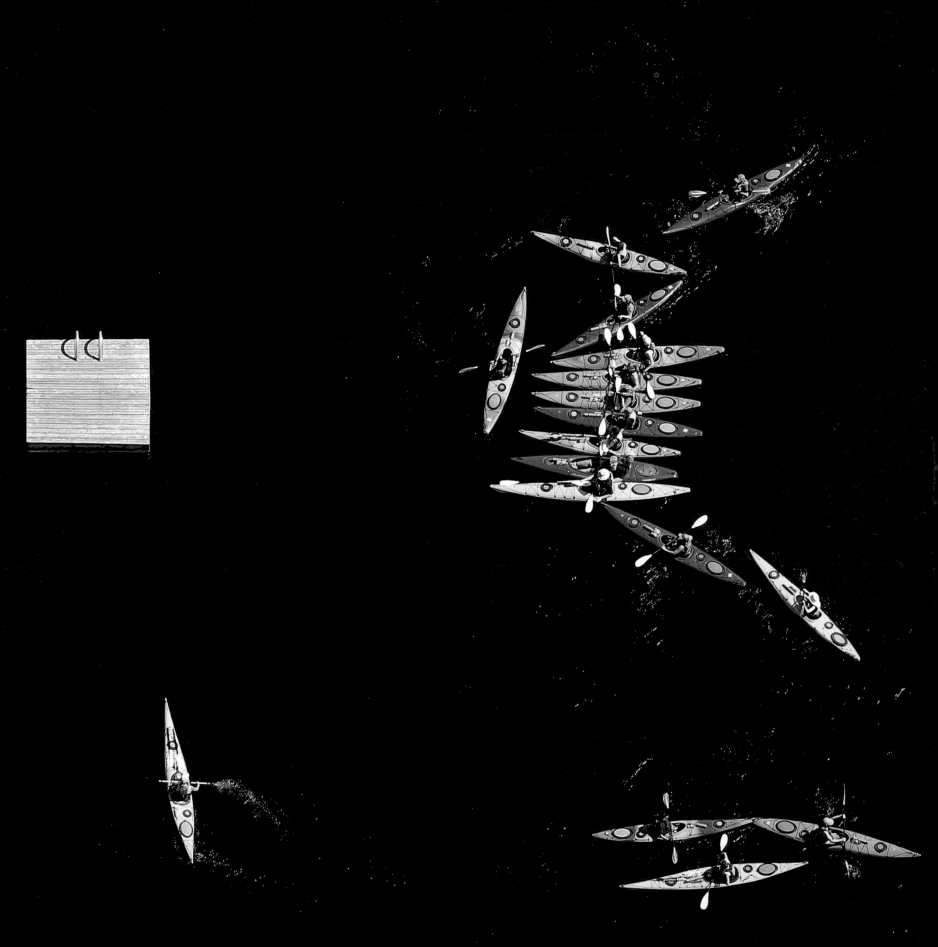

A secluded shoreline shows off an artistic natural design.

Reflections of fall trees against a crisp blue sky paint a pond in vibrant colours. As the leaves turn from green to gold and red, they attract weekend trippers searching for spectacular displays.

ALGONQUIN PARK, WHITNEY

Getting my "skate legs" back on the first ice of the season makes me feel like I'm part of winter.

The season is too long not to embrace its charms.

—George Fischer

Every year, more than a million visitors don their
skates for a spin on the world's longest skating rink
(equal to 90 Olympic-sized rinks). Also used by city
commuters, the 7.8 kilometres from Dow Lake to
the National Arts Centre along the Rideau Canal are
dotted with snack stands and souvenir shacks.

OTTAWA

During the late 1800s, fishing guides used
St. Lawrence River Skiffs to row clients out to
well-stocked fishing spots. The flat-bottomed boats
provide stability in changing river conditions, and
are easy to pull onto beaches for picnics.

IVY LEA, LANSDOWNE

You're never too young to ride the Muskoka chairs
and chill out on Joel Stone Beach.

GANANOQUE

Ontario boasts about 550 wildflower species and more than 2700 flowering plants. Most are native, while others were brought by European settlers or were accidentally imported in ships' cargo holds or on trains, clothing or mud-caked boots.

Ontario backroads are an enchanting world. Trails offer secluded, quiet paths, logging roads and prime spots off the beaten track. Walking and cycling are popular modes of exploration.

NEAR GAMEBRIDGE

Wilderness beauty flies by on the train to Agawa
Canyon from Sault Ste. Marie, one of North America's
oldest settlements.

NORTH OF SAULT STE. MARIE

FOLLOWING PAGES
Early morning glow surrounds the dunes at
Sandbanks Provincial Park. The popular park has been
the location for several movie shoots, including *Fly
Away Home* (1996) and *Resident Evil: Afterlife* (2010).

PICTON

The Canadian Pacific Railway connected the country with communications and transportation during the late 1800s, although dangerous and harsh conditions during the building phase exacted a high price on labourers' lives. Settlements grew around the rails and their branch lines.

NEAR SAULT STE. MARIE

Snow and ice sculpt a unique temporary scene.

City Hall is seen through a snow-packed castle arch
during Feb Fest, dubbed "a flurry of fantastic fun."

KINGSTON

The lens captures the energy of the Credit River as it
rushes by in a blur.

FORKS OF THE CREDIT

Conquering the challenging river on a wakeboard adds to summer fun. Combining water skiing, snowboarding and surfing, the sport has been part of the World Games since 2005.

NEAR BROCKVILLE

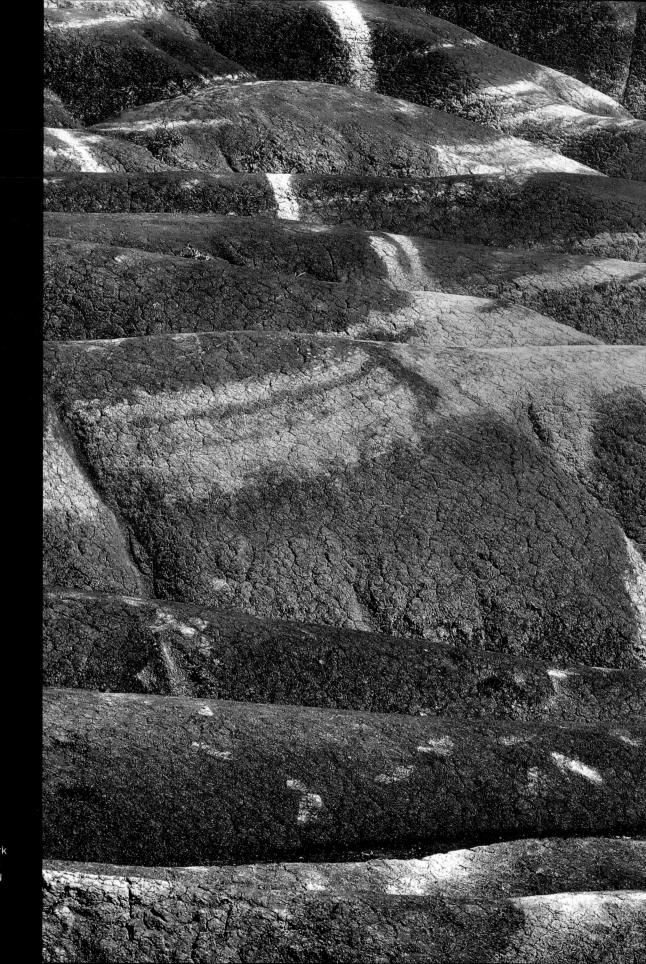

Rolling mounds of Queenston shale are a hallmark of the Cheltenham Badlands. This rare site, cared for by the Bruce Trail Association, is regulated by law to preserve its integrity.

CHELTENHAM

A small stand of trees defines the horizon along the
dunes in Sandbanks Provincial Park. The trees are
part of a 1921 reforestation project, spearheaded by
the provincial government, to stabilize the dunes.

One of the Thousand Islands emerges in soft pastels
on a misty morning in the narrows.

PICTON

NEAR BROCKVILLE

A winter freeze dramatically changes the feel of a
waterfall as shapes merge into natural sculptures.
Louth Falls is just starting its seasonal transformation
as cold September winds take control.

LOUTH

Canada will be
a strong country
when Canadians
of all provinces
feel at home in
all parts of the
country, and when
they feel that all
Canada belongs
to them.

—Pierre Elliott Trudeau, former Prime Minister of Canada

Fiddleheads prefer growing in damp ground by rivers or streams. A tasty delicacy, they can be boiled or steamed, as well as seasoned with butter, garlic and spices.

A winding river pushes its way through the verdant
boreal forest, which comprises two-thirds of the
province's 50 million hectares of woodland.

NORTHERN ONTARIO

Reeds create an abstract pattern along the shore of
Twelve Mile Bay.

GEORGIAN BAY

The Gardiner Expressway, completed in 1966, runs close to the shore of Lake Ontario. It was built in sections, with several overpasses.

TORONTO

Inspired by the Taj Mahal, Thomas Foster built a Christian memorial temple for his family incorporating the apostles and gospel writers. Four great arches and marble columns house three crypts.

UXBRIDGE

moments
in Culture

Ontario is not only Canada's most populous province, but also the country's most diverse, with more than 25 percent of its residents born outside our borders. The people of Toronto – Canada's largest city – comprise 200 distinct ethnic origins. Almost 30 percent of those are from Europe.

As a Hungarian-Canadian who married a Canadian and whose children are native Canadians, I am a good example of an immigrant who introduced a different culture, yet integrated successfully into my adopted country. My family, which fled Hungary during the 1956 revolution, brought along a strong work ethic, solid values and many talents. For example, when I became an accountant, my parents were pleased that I had entered a reputable, no-nonsense profession. But they were puzzled when I changed my career to photographer and began to hang out of planes, skitter down cliffs and scale mountains to get the perfect shots. They also passed down a love of travel and an acceptance of diversity:

I speak English, French and Hungarian, while my two sons are bilingual.

My Toronto gallery on Queen Street West is in the heart of a multicultural district founded in the 19th century. Just down the street from Kensington Market – arguably the city's most diverse neighbourhood – it is flanked by a jazz club and a Japanese restaurant. Across the street is a tattoo parlour and a fancy cooking school. Short walks in either direction lead to graffiti-adorned alleys and international hotel chains.

Ontario celebrates this diversity year round with hundreds of festivals and events – from ribfests to theatre, dancing and music. Throughout the province, First Nation powwows abound. Colourful War of 1812 re-enactments recall the British Loyalists. Kitchener hosts the second-largest Oktoberfest in the world. And the common threads are inclusivity, pride and freedom.

Lively sounds around eclectic shops with myriad bargains, independent cafés and unique markets comprise the multicultural Kensington Market neighbourhood, which traces its roots back to the 1920s.

TORONTO

A lot of "2112" was written in the back seat of a car and in cold dressing rooms while on tour in northern Ontario.

—Alex Lifeson, Rush guitarist, native of Toronto

Jazz tunes filter through the night breeze from the Rex Hotel. This family-owned jazz and blues mecca has been a fixture on Queen Street since the 20th century.

TORONTO

Dancers rock to the beat of the annual Toronto
Caribbean Carnival (a.k.a. Caribana). The festival
began as a one-time celebration in 1967 but quickly
became wildly popular.

TORONTO

Named after the chute that diverted logs past
the waterfalls at the turn of the century, Chutes
Provincial Park contains a series of impressive rapids
and falls along the Aux Sables River.

MASSEY

Surrounding the Slovak Cathedral of Transfiguration, the 200-acre Cathedraltown settlement was initiated in 2006. The vision, still to be completed, includes shops, a European-style piazza and parks.

MARKHAM

Colours reflected from the hull of a Centre Island ferry dance in the ripples on Lake Ontario.

TORONTO

With more than 250,000 lakes, finding a diving spot has long been a popular pastime.

SUGAR ISLAND, GEORGIAN BAY

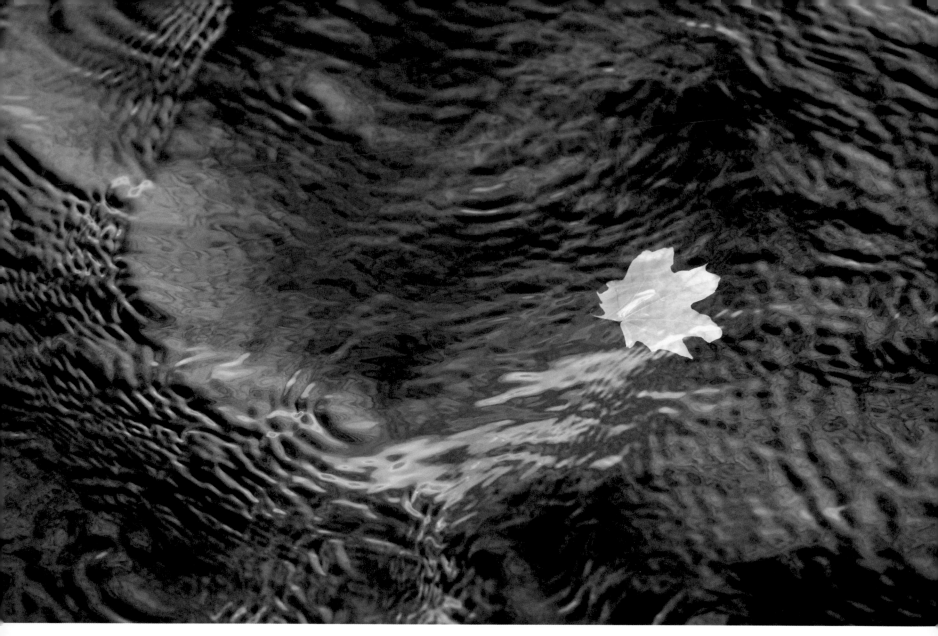

The river's moods can create gentle waves that allow
paddlers to meander, or become rushing currents that
hustle boats along in a blur.

THE THOUSAND ISLANDS

Dragon boat racing draws international crowds that
enjoy related events in many cities (Canada geese
not included).

TORONTO

Bold colours on traditional Muskoka chairs
encourage visitors to stop and stay a while.

Now used for cadet programs and some private enterprises, Canadian Forces Base Picton was built as a wartime training installation. It was a dynamic hub from 1938 to 1969.

PICTON

FOLLOWING PAGES

Ancient white cedars cling to soaring cliffs on the Niagara Escarpment on Georgian Bay. Incredible vistas reward hikers visiting Lion's Head Provincial Nature Reserve. Nearby, the Bruce Trail passes the Tobermory trailhead, then runs 885 kilometres to Queenston.

LION'S HEAD

Vegetation clings to a granite outcrop.

Close to urban development but surrounded by a woodlot in the Vinemount Moraine, Felkers Falls cascades over a 20-metre precipice to fascinating rock layers at its base.

Beautiful lines on sleek runabouts hold perennial
allure for many Thousand Islanders, who love to zoom
along the St. Lawrence River.

NEAR KINGSTON

A British soldier takes aim in a Fort Wellington military drill reenactment. The fortification originally protected the St. Lawrence River shipping route from attack by the U.S. during the War of 1812 and helped foil the American invasion of Upper and Lower Canada between 1837 and 1838.

PRESCOTT

A well-weathered post fence outlines a farmer's field.

SOUTHERN ONTARIO

A small stand of gray birches filters the sunlight. The trees were initially more prevalent in eastern Canada, but are spreading west and north.

The maples are about all stripped of leaves now, but the birches are very rich in colour...

—Tom Thomson, Group of Seven artist, native of Claremont

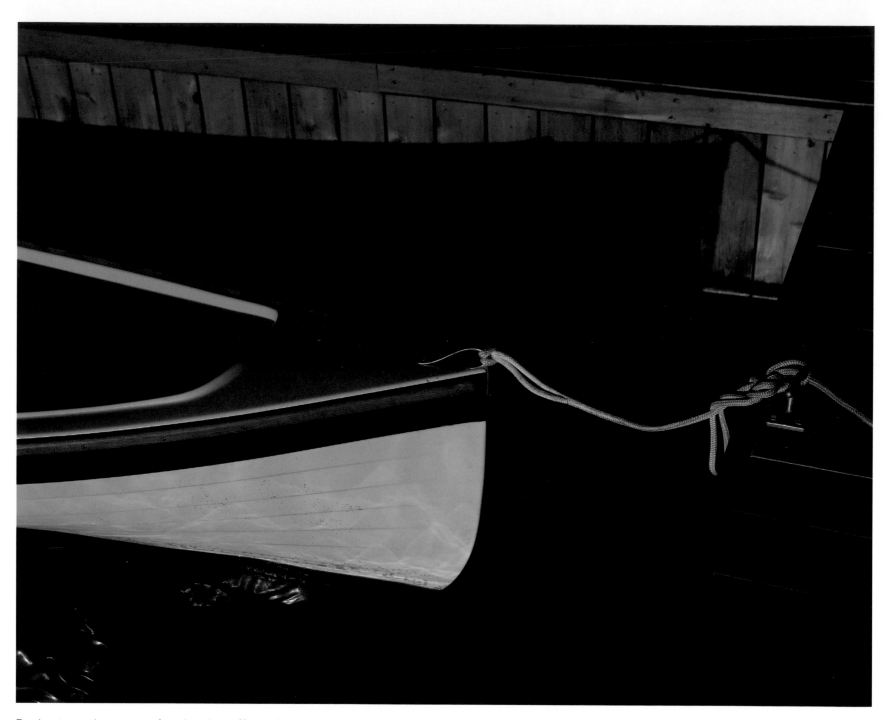

Rowboats may be commonplace, but they offer each
paddler unique adventures.

Ontario's Carolinian zone along the shores of
Lake Erie is classified as a humid continental climatic
zone. This important agricultural area is home to
species not found elsewhere at this latitude.

POINT PELEE

Now part of Lang
Pioneer Village, Lang Mill
produced up to 8000
barrels of flour annually
during its heyday in the
mid–1800s. Powered
by the Indian River, its
working turbine is set
inside the mill.

KEENE

Glaze ice frames an emergency life preserver with a rugged design.

LAKE SIMCOE

Built in Ameliasburg in 1842, Roblin's Mill was moved to Black Creek Pioneer Village in 1964 and is Toronto's only operating stone mill. The functional water wheel idea can be traced back to third-century Greece.

TORONTO

Deciduous trees brave the January cold and wait
patiently for the return of spring.

ORILLIA

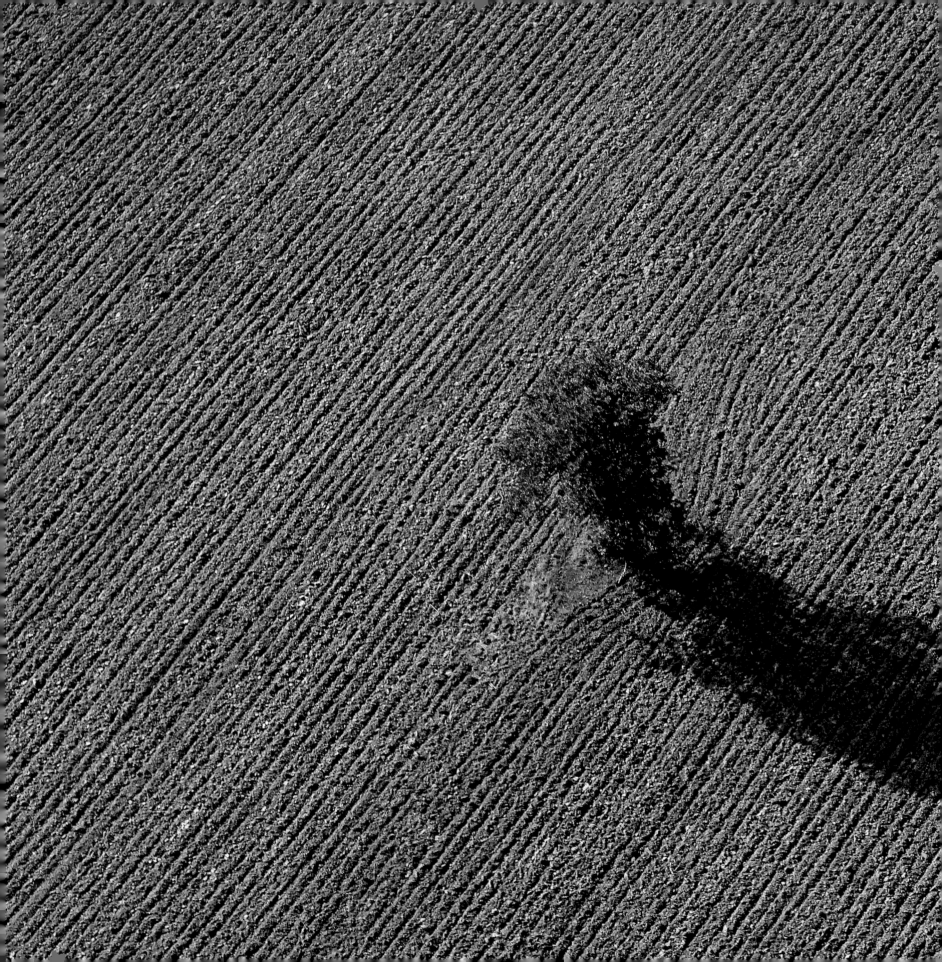

A lone tree takes a stand in a well-tilled field on the largest of the Thousand Islands.

WOLFE ISLAND

Cycling is a scenic option for exploring on more personal terms. Hundreds of kilometres of trails pass through forests, shorelines or rails for a memorable trip.

PEFFERLAW

The first glimpse
of a white veil of
water never fails
to inspire me.

—George Fischer

Bridal Veil Falls plunges prettily for about 12 metres over limestone. It is a restful spot for cooling off in the pool or under the "veil" after exploring nearby trails, the town on Mudge Bay and the pulp mill.

KAGAWONG

From the shore of Nine Mile Point you can look
across the length of Lake Ontario.

SIMCOE ISLAND

The CN Tower's EdgeWalk, an urban adventure
356 metres above ground, is the thrill of a lifetime
(safety equipment provided).

TORONTO

The Centennial Flame commemorating Canada's
Confederation burns in front of the Peace Tower on
Parliament Hill.

OTTAWA

You miss 100%
of the shots
you don't take.

—Wayne Gretzky, NHL athlete, native of Brantford

The epitome of a Canadian getaway, camping under
the night sky is an experience to treasure.

THE THOUSAND ISLANDS

A beautiful historic home with a festive feel
dominates the street.

KINGSTON

Lauded for its magnificent restoration, the Old Stone Mill is a wonderful example of a fully automatic gristmill from the Upper Canada era. Built in 1810, it is now in the care of The Delta Mill Society.

DELTA

Cotton grass finds a good place to grow in the boggy area of a field. These hardy perennials, believed to be medicinal, have been used for candlewicks, pillow stuffing and wound dressings.

RIDEAU LAKES

The colourful last crop of the season delights
farmers' market shoppers.

LEEDS GRENVILLE

Serene scenic layers take shape in the early
morning light.

NEAR KINGSTON

Two of the city's familiar sights embrace in a blur.

TORONTO

First settled in 1785, Elizabethtown was renamed
Brockville in 1812 to honour General Isaac Brock.

BROCKVILLE

Viewed from the CN Tower, downtown skyscrapers
light up the night.

TORONTO

The rhythm
of waves has
an energy that
puts things into
perspective.

—George Fischer

A weathered tree faces the evening light on Lake Simcoe. Its original Wyandot (Huron) name was *Ouentironk* ("Beautiful Water") and later *Lake Toronto*, but John Graves Simcoe, British army officer and first Lieutenant Governor of Upper Canada, renamed it for his late father.

The winter sun casts dark shadows onto the dock at
Lake Couchiching, a popular all-season fishing spot.

NEAR ORILLIA

A paper birch sheds its bark, providing an important
winter food source for a number of forest animals.

Spring is a time of renewal. The air is laden with the colours and aromas of blossom trees, fresh grass and mouth-watering fruit.

—George Fischer

Best cultivated in a cool, moist climate, strawberries find Southern Ontario a perfect growing area. A member of the rose family, they are at their best in June or July when you can buy baskets of them from the growers — or pick your own.

Built in 1872, the Morningstar Mill is powered by the
river flowing into DeCew Falls. It has been restored by
the Friends of Morningstar Mill.

ST. CATHARINES

Historic wooden boats are a popular means of
transportation in the Thousand Islands.
Well-maintained and in pristine condition, many
also grace classic boat shows.

THE THOUSAND ISLANDS

moments
in Nature

In Ontario, each of the four seasons is a gem. As I cycle the backroads around my country getaway north of Toronto, I'm met by vibrant scenery and delightful scents. In spring, lilacs and fruit blossoms and jasmine greet me, while summer is marked by sweetgrass and lavender and roses. Fall fragrances emanate from leaves on the ground in Muskoka, grapes in wine country and bonfires in campgrounds. Festivals such as Winterlude in Ottawa bring memories of skating on the Rideau Canal, where the air is punctuated with the aroma of tasty BeaverTails and hot chocolate.

Summer moments for me are about sinking my toes into the rolling dunes of Sandbanks Provincial Park or the pillowy beaches at Long Point – and disturbing the peace on Georgian Bay by cannonballing off the deck into the water during our men's weekends. They are about early-morning mists rising from the lake around my canoe, and the haunting loon calls in Algonquin Park.

During the two years of collecting images for my Ontario book on waterfalls, I was astonished by the quantity and variety of falls in the area. Their distant roar is music to my ears, while the bracing spray of Niagara Falls invigorates my face. (When I'm shooting photos, however, I hide myself and my gear behind plastic sheets and chuckle as tourists discover the raw power of Niagara on boat tours into the abyss.)

In fall, I love to crash through harvested cornfields to the rustling of dry stalks – and take some home to decorate the porch. In winter, the clatter of ice skates on frozen ponds recalls the days of my childhood. And every spring the cycle starts anew.

ONTARIO'S PROTECTED AREAS SUMMARY

Provincial Protected Area	No.	Hectares	% of Prov.
Regulated Provincial Parks	334	7,905,305	7.4%
Regulated Conservation Reserves	295	1,514,147	1.4%
Dedicated Protected Areas – Regulated under PPCRA	5	349,481	0.3%
Dedicated Protected Areas – Non-regulated	4	876,535	0.8%
Wilderness Areas	11	838	<0.1%
Total Provincial Protected Areas	649	10,646,306	10%
National Parks	5	208,160	0.2%
Total National and Provincial Protected Areas	654	10,854,466	10.2%

ONTARIO LAKES WITH AREA MORE THAN 400 km²

Lake	Area (including islands)
Lake Superior	82,100 km²
Lake Huron	59,600 km²
Lake Erie	25,700 km²
Lake Ontario	18,960 km²
Lake Nipigon	4,848 km²
Lake of the Woods	3,150 km²
Lac Seul	1,657 km²
Lake St. Clair	1,114 km²
Rainy Lake	932 km²
Lake Abitibi	931 km²
Lake Nipissing	832 km²
Lake Simcoe	744 km²
Big Trout Lake	661 km²
Sandy Lake	527 km²
Lake St. Joseph	493 km²
Trout Lake	413 km²

PROVINCIAL STATS

Number of lakes	over 250,000
Number of farms	approx. 51,950
Number of trees	approx. 85 billion
Forested area	66% (70 million hectares)

The iconic trillium is Ontario's protected provincial flower.

The Rideau River drops to meet the Ottawa River
from two high cliffs separated by Green Island.
Important during the mid-1800s for its hydropower,
this spot was redeveloped into Rideau Falls Park after
World War II.

OTTAWA

FOLLOWING PAGES
Sea stacks that resemble flowerpots created an
identity for the two-square-kilometre area of
Flowerpot Island. Accessible only by boat, it is part of
Fathom Five National Marine Park.

TOBERMORY

Lily pads are almost obscured by the rippling reflection of trees. They grow in peaceful ponds, providing natural oxygen, shade and shelter for fish.

It is to be observed that "angling" is the name given to fishing by people who can't fish.

—Stephen Leacock, author, Ontario resident

On the same latitude as northern California, the north shore of Lake Erie enjoys a long growing season and some of the nation's most fertile soil.

LEAMINGTON

Thanks to the sandbars, this phenomenal
11-kilometre stretch of freshwater beach offers
shallow, warm waters.

SAUBLE BEACH

Joel Stone Beach, on the shore of the St. Lawrence River, is the perfect place to slow down and enjoy the summer.

GANANOQUE

Summer's tall grasses blur as they sway in an
abstract dance.

Able to thrive in moist soil, tiger day lilies grow everywhere, from hills and valleys to roadsides and ditches. Sometimes seen as an invasive species, they are nicknamed "ditch lily."

THE THOUSAND ISLANDS

Every sunset sky takes on a unique luminescence.

—George Fischer

The sun sets on Lake Ontario's shoreline at Mimico, established in 1905.

ETOBICOKE

Warm hues saturate the leaves as the days get shorter and trees prepare for winter. Fall colours attract hordes of sightseers.

ALGONQUIN PROVINCIAL PARK

Ontario boasts some of the world's best fishing,
whether it's in cold-water rivers, wilderness streams
or an ice-fishing hut on a frozen lake.

HALIBURTON

Shadows emphasize the contours of snow drifts, a
common sight in the short days of an Ontario winter.

The treacherous rocks in the Main Duck Island shipping channel have claimed countless ships and lives. According to one legend, in 1760 two French crews were shipwrecked here and buried their gold in the harbour. It has never been found.

THOUSAND ISLANDS NATIONAL PARK

A flash freeze creates sheets of ice on the St. Lawrence
River, reminding us that nature rules.

THE THOUSAND ISLANDS

The *Pride of Baltimore* in full sail along the
St. Lawrence Seaway during its goodwill summer
cruise through the Great Lakes.

NEAR BROCKVILLE

Marking the border of Ontario and New York State,
the Niagara River surges over the American Falls
and the Canadian Horseshoe Falls (shown here),
both dropping roughly 57 metres. The combination
of height and volume makes Niagara Falls one of the
world's most popular tourist attractions.

NIAGARA FALLS

FOLLOWING PAGES
With a luminous evening glow, the Michael Lee-Chin
Crystal marks the entrance to the Royal Ontario
Museum (ROM), Canada's largest museum.

TORONTO

FAMILY
FUN
WEEKENDS

April, May, June

Eager for spring thaw, a row of boats at Lagoon City
push their bows out from under winter shelter.

BRECHIN

Settled in the late 1700s, the townships around Lake Erie have a colourful history — taking in fugitive slaves from the U.S.A. in the 1800s, surviving fires, political strife, a tollgate rebellion and a railway explosion. The region is now an important agricultural district.

NEAR ESSEX

A key communications tool, the dinner bell called workers scattered across the farm to gather for a hot meal.

BEAVERTON

Beautiful Black Angus cattle pose for the camera. This docile and hardy English breed produces top-quality beef.

NEAR ARISS

Anyone who has known Algonquin Park will be disappointed when they get to Heaven.

—Ralph Bice, trapper and guide

Steam rises from a warm pond as cold air moves over it.

ALGONQUIN PARK, WHITNEY

Take your snow boots out for Ontario winter recreation: downhill or cross-country skiing, boarding, tubing or tobogganing.

BLUE MOUNTAIN, COLLINGWOOD

Like sentinels of past lives, ghostly buildings with
stories to tell dot the landscape.

NEAR OWEN SOUND

Fashioned in the High Victorian Gothic Revival style, Belleville City Hall features a 44-metre clock tower. The building was completed in 1873 during an economic depression as a symbol of civic pride and confidence in the future.

BELLEVILLE

The light at False Duck Island (also known as Swetman Island) is marked by red and white bands. The original tower, established in 1828, is now part of the Mariners Park Marine Museum; the new tower was built in 1965.

MILFORD

Calm blue water reflects the passionate hues of
an antique boat, representing an intriguing part of
maritime romance.

THE THOUSAND ISLANDS

FOLLOWING PAGES
The Humber Bay Bridge for pedestrian and
bicycle traffic connects a series of parks along the
lakeshore in Etobicoke.

TORONTO

Lake Michigan, a 223-metre Great Lakes ship, is one of the largest cargo freighters serving the St. Lawrence Seaway system. Ships travelling on the upper lakes can be as long as 305 metres. However, the maximum allowable length for vessels using the Seaway between Montreal and Lake Erie is 230 metres as the locks are only 233 metres long.

NEAR RESORT ISLAND

An aerial view of a community covered in snow evokes needlepoint stitching.

OTTAWA

Some of the Duchesnay Falls' low cascades surge into two channels and a number of scenic waterfalls. The lower falls drops approximately eight to 10 metres while the upper falls descends over a 20-metre "staircase."

NORTH BAY

Discovering the tracks of an early bird is a treat in
Sandbanks Provincial Park.

PICTON

Signs of summer include excited fans watching
Ontario's baseball team, the Blue Jays, at the
Rogers Centre.

TORONTO

FOLLOWING PAGES
Corn is a versatile crop, providing a favourite seasonal
dish, corn on the cob. Dried stalks after the harvest
are used for animal feed, marshmallows, toothpaste,
fireworks — even biofuel.

NEAR ORILLIA

Early buds, assaulted by a late freeze, generally survive brief drops in temperature as spring fights its way in.

Muskoka chairs linger on a cottage deck, envisioning
summer sun and activity on the lake.

BRECHIN

Artists find a multitude of inspirational subjects to expand their creativity and pursue their passion.

THE THOUSAND ISLANDS

Ontario vineyards produce world-class wines, including icewine and sparkling wine. Fruit wine is also popular, as are libations made from maple syrup or honey.

moments in Art

Trekking through the wilderness of this great province is always inspirational. Giant pine trees bowing to the wind and intricately textured rock strata built over centuries remind me of the colourful, abstract paintings of the Group of Seven, the most important Canadian artists of the early 20th century. Their art gave the world new impressions of our astounding Canadian Shield, boreal forest and shimmering waters.

My love of art has led to some interesting experiences, and it is a family affair. Over the years, my wife and I have turned the walls of our house and cottage into a visual feast of art collected here and around the world. Aboriginal creations are a particular passion of mine, and I have walls and niches dedicated to such paintings and sculptures. In fact, with my assistant and friend, Jean, I have gone so far as to build a totem pole at my cottage that symbolizes my spiritual connection to Native culture.

Throughout Ontario, I am surrounded by artists and artisans from today and yesterday. In Orillia near my cottage is a memorial to Gordon Lightfoot, the Canadian singer-songwriter who helped define the folk-pop sound of the 1960s and '70s and continues to enthrall audiences everywhere. Orillia was also an inspiration to author Stephen Leacock, whose summer house there is now a National Historic Site.

Highlighting the immense craftsmanship that we have to offer the world are Toronto's One of a Kind Show and Sale as well as the sales of handmade Mennonite quilts. Yes, Ontario's great environment encourages fresh thinking and rich creativity. And it is a testament to the abundantly creative spirit.

One of the largest art museums in North America, the Art Gallery of Ontario (AGO) boasts a collection of more than 90,000 works.

TORONTO

Richly costumed Shakespearean actors entertain passersby in an historical setting. Theatre performances along with Medieval and Renaissance fairs and festivals, create fantasy worlds for those wanting to escape the present for a short while.

BROCKVILLE

Joel Stone Beach provides numerous opportunities to kick up your heels with friends.

GANANOQUE

Sunflowers in the budding stage turn their faces to the sun. Ontario sunflowers are generally used for birdseed and confectionery.

Boats are the transport of choice on the St. Lawrence
River. The river flows 1197 kilometres from Lake
Ontario into the Gulf of St. Lawrence.

Designs from wind and currents play in the water around small islands near Crab Cove, one of the many spots known for great fishing around "The Bruce."

BRUCE PENINSULA

Unspoiled nature shelters Brooks Falls, a surprisingly accessible cascade.

EMSDALE

A familiar rural site, a mailbox lineup faces the roadside. The federal government has handled postal service since 1868.

PREVIOUS PAGES

The largest group of fresh-water islands in the world, Georgian Bay's 30,000 Islands were discovered by tourists in the late 1800s. While rocks often make the waters treacherous, the area offers some of the world's greatest cruising.

GEORGIAN BAY

Connecting Indian Lake and Opinicon Lake over a four-metre height variation, Chaffeys Lock 37 is named for Samuel Chaffey who set up the local Grist Mill, Saw Mill, Fulling and Carding and distillery around 1820.

RIDEAU LAKES

The Thousand Islands Bridge system is a series of five bridges connecting northern New York in the United States with southeastern Ontario in Canada. The Canadian span of the Thousand Islands Bridge system is 1015 metres.

NEAR LANSDOWNE

Biker culture has something for everyone. Ontario has the most motorcycle clubs in the nation and requires motorcycle licences.

With their gentle ways and loyal souls, horses are popular pets. Some industries are returning to horsepower in an effort to reduce damage to the environment caused by heavy equipment.

NEAR GLENORA

Completely at the whim of the current, leaves surf over the precipice of the rapids adding colour to the white water.

The *MS Chi-Cheemaun* passenger and car ferry passes Echo Island. From May to October, it sails 40 kilometres to connect Tobermory and South Baymouth in just under two hours.

BETWEEN BRUCE PENINSULA AND
MANITOULIN ISLAND

Winter ice storms never fail to elicit a sense of awe as they turn the landscape into surreal scenes.

NEAR BEAVERTON

Abandoned as an air base decades ago, Canadian
Forces Base Picton has the feel of a ghost town. The
authentic set was used by CBC for its made-for-TV
movie *Dieppe*.

PICTON

Built in 1936 as a carding mill, Hope Sawmill was
expanded in 1873 to focus on sawmilling. Restored to
working condition, it sits in a picturesque area close to
the Hope Mill Conservation Area.

LANG

Twenty different varieties of apples are grown in
Ontario, mainly along the southern stretches. The
crisp, nutritious fruit provides a high-fibre, low-fat
snack. It is amazingly versatile and delicious raw or
baked, sauced, simmered, grilled or frozen. Apples add
special flavour to pies, cobblers, crumbles, salads, ice
cream and dumplings.

Views from an abandoned farmhouse remind us
that life moves on.

GILBERT MILLS

Agricultural fields and greenhouses (the largest concentration in North America) contribute to the geometric landscape in this very fertile region that grows mainly tomatoes, peppers, cucumbers and flowers.

LEAMINGTON

PREVIOUS PAGES

Cove Island Lighthouse, automated since 1991, helps mark the passage from Tobermory to South Baymouth. It was the first lighthouse fired up on Georgian Bay in 1858, and the last to have had a keeper.

FATHOM FIVE NATIONAL MARINE PARK, BRUCE PENINSULA

From the mainland to Howe Island, the *Frontenac–Howe Islander* ferries passengers and their cars year round, 24 hours a day. The vessel's operating history dates back to 1898. It is now owned by the Ontario Ministry of Transportation and operated by the County of Frontenac.

KINGSTON

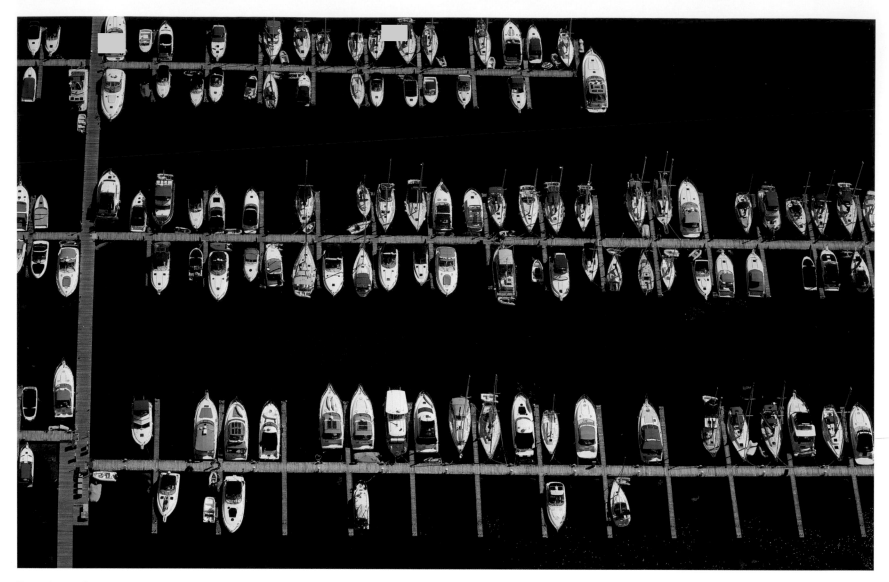

Boats in the Gananoque Municipal Marina create a
floating matrix. The popular 385-slip shelter offers
sailors various services.

GANANOQUE

Huckleberry Island is a good place to relax and observe nature.

An exhilarating diving destination, the Thousand Islands Region is acclaimed for its water clarity, marine life and seascapes. Explorers can discover shipwrecks from as far back as 1812 that were lost on the historic trade route.

THE THOUSAND ISLANDS

An aerial view displays the underwater landscape near Whiskey Harbour, a thrilling backyard for those living in the area.

NORTHERN BRUCE PENINSULA

A very different vista in the winter, the profile of
Sugar Island is typical of many of the 30,000 Islands.

GEORGIAN BAY

Frozen on the river, a tiny house battles the whipping winds. The St. Lawrence River normally freezes over from December to March.

THE THOUSAND ISLANDS

Casa Loma, a unique landmark built between 1911 and 1914
for financier Sir Henry Pellatt, was never totally completed.
However, its 98 rooms, secret passageways and stables
made it the largest private home at the time. In 1923,
Pellatt lost his magnum opus due to financial difficulties.
The City seized it in 1933 for back taxes and has been
leasing it out as an event venue and public museum.

TORONTO

The McMichael Canadian Art Collection is an important part of Ontario's cultural landscape. Established in the mid–20th century, it is a national treasure showcasing Canadian art and providing unique educational insights. The gallery is renowned for its collections of the Group of Seven and contemporaries as well as First Nation, Métis and Inuit art.

KLEINBURG

Shards of ice buckle skyward against waves that continue pushing the frozen lake against the shore.

NEAR ATHERLY

A patchwork of fields provides a sharp contrast to the
rugged cliffs across the narrow inlet of Irish Harbour
near Black Creek Provincial Park.

BRUCE PENINSULA

FOLLOWING PAGES
January chill creates a misty effect where air and
water fight for dominance. Best viewed from a comfy
armchair beside a fireplace.

THE THOUSAND ISLANDS

The Ferguson Gristmill operated from 1857 to 1940 on the Rocky Saugeen River. The charming building is now a private residence.

NEAR DURHAM

A quick elevator ride to the observation decks on the
1000 Islands Tower sends visitors up 130 metres to
observe the panorama from on high.

LANSDOWNE

A familiar sight on farms around the province, clusters
of tall, sturdy silos provide storage for livestock feed.

CALEDON

Excitement
peaks with
the smell of
popcorn
and candy
at the CNE.

—George Fischer

The Canadian National Exhibition (CNE) has been
Canada's "showcase" since it was founded in 1879. The
fair attracts about 1.5 million visitors annually over its
18 days of rides, games, music and exhibits, and
employs roughly 5000 youth.

TORONTO

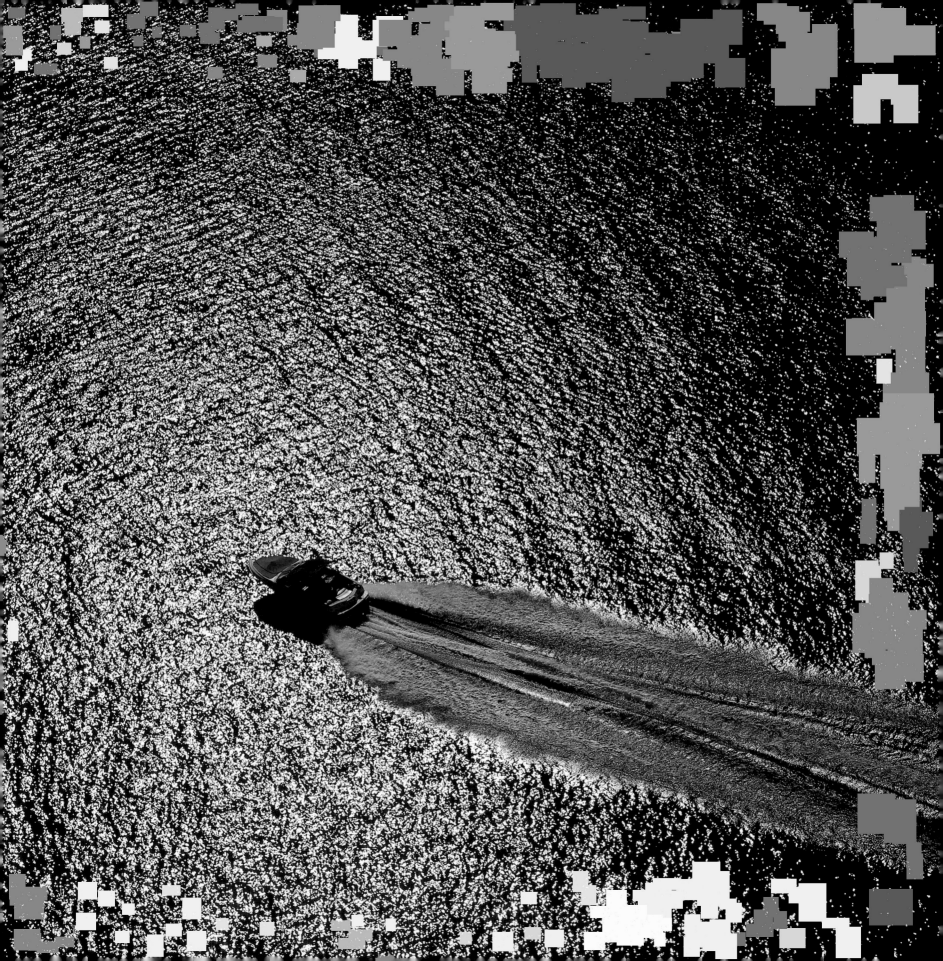

The bright yellow flowers of a canola crop catch the last rays of the day. Cholesterol-free and high in vitamin E, canola oil's light, clear properties make it the choice of many chefs.

NEAR BLUE MOUNTAIN

PREVIOUS PAGES
A unique steel-frame light tower watches over Pigeon Island. The stairway to the light and the watch room runs up the steel tube in the centre of the frame.

NEAR WOLFE ISLAND

A runabout rushes along to make port before the sun sets.

THE THOUSAND ISLANDS

Washboard Falls cascades five metres down the rough surface and continues on to Tiffany Falls farther downstream. While visitors can view the falls from below, the property above is private.

DUNDAS

Mature tree bark creates an interesting texture.

PREVIOUS PAGES
Viewed from the west part of the city, the silhouettes
of downtown buildings sculpt distinctive shapes.
Toronto is the most populous city in Canada and a
prominent international centre for business, art
and culture.

TORONTO

Middle Island is Canada's southernmost point, roughly
parallel to Barcelona, Spain and Rome, Italy.

POINT PELEE

For more than 202 kilometres, the Rideau Canal Links the Ottawa River to Lake Ontario at Kingston. The popular skating portion in Ottawa is flooded at night by city workers who drill holes in the ice that pump water upwards to smooth the surface.

OTTAWA

Ice-fishing basics include your gear and a hole in the ice. However, for a more comfortable experience, you can use an ice hut towed onto the ice every season as the lake freezes over. Some huts even have satellite TV and stocked fridges.

LAKE SIMCOE

Protecting the southwest shore of Simcoe Island
(named for John Graves Simcoe), Nine Mile
Point Lighthouse has a commanding view of the
St. Lawrence River. Built in 1833 and automated
in 1978, the light shines from a height of almost
14 metres.

SIMCOE ISLAND

Canadians still spend so
much time discussing what it
means to be Canadian.

—Dave Foley, native of Etobicoke

Four gargoyles survey the city from the Old City Hall
clock tower. The tower is 103.6 metres high and until
1917 was the tallest structure in Canada.

TORONTO

Tunnel lights help create a feeling of movement on a
Toronto Transit Commission (TTC) subway.

TORONTO

Intriguing detail and Romanesque style define Old City Hall. Constructed over the decade between 1889 and 1899 and replaced by the current City Hall in 1965, it now serves as a courthouse.

TORONTO

The unique architecture of the Caledonia Mill boasts three-and one-half storeys plus basement and a decorative cupola. It began milling wheat into flour in 1857 and closed in 1966, becoming the last mill powered by water along the Grand River.

CALEDONIA

FOLLOWING PAGES

Wonderfully crafted at the turn of the 20th century, the Canadian Niagara Power Bridge has five spans, each over 90 metres long. The Niagara power plants are the largest generators of hydroelectric power in North America.

NIAGARA FALLS

moments
in Trade

From my photography studio in Toronto's quirky Queen West neighbourhood, I absorb the intense sights, sounds and flavours of Ontario's capital city. Fashionistas stroll by, having gorged on shopping in the Art and Design District. Jazz aficionados hang at the Rex Hotel Jazz & Blues Bar, while busy restaurants and food trucks send whiffs of garlic and curry and BBQ up to my door. Everywhere you look, business is being conducted.

I also enjoy gazing up at Toronto's brilliant cathedrals of commerce such as First Canadian Place, Brookfield Place and its Allen Lambert Galleria. When the mood strikes, I can stroll to Bay Street, the heart of the country's financial system, the iconic CN Tower on Front Street, or to the internationally renowned Theatre District on King.

While Toronto is Canada's largest city and a hub of financial activity, other cities play important roles as well. Ottawa is the nation's capital; London is a regional centre of healthcare and education. Waterloo is now part of the 100-km Toronto-Waterloo Region Corridor – the second-largest technology cluster in North America.

Ontario is also home to much of Canada's best agricultural land. The fertile soil yields crops such as soybeans, corn, wheat, fruit and vegetables – and in the south nurtures orchards, grapevines and Carolinian forests. At countless farmers' markets across the province, I can stock up on fresh produce as well as beef, pork, lamb and fowl in true field-to-table style.

Ontario also produces the most metals in Canada and is the leading manufacturing province. The Big Nickel in Sudbury is a reminder of Ontario's rich ore deposits, while Sarnia's Chemical Valley is home to more than 60 refineries and chemical plants. I'm pleased to see new biotechnology companies moving into the area to turn agricultural and forestry waste into sustainable chemicals and clean energy.

Putting their skills to the test, lumberjacks face off throughout the day on various competitive events for cash prizes and bragging rights.

BEAVERTON

"Good things come to those who bait." The Ontario Ministry of Natural Resources and Forestry reports that 1.27 million anglers fish in Ontario each year.

The low, terraced Sauble Falls welcomes rainbow trout and Chinook salmon returning for their spring and fall spawning runs. Visitors can watch from a boardwalk as the fish struggle against the current and leap onto the ledges on their journey upstream.

SOUTH BRUCE PENINSULA

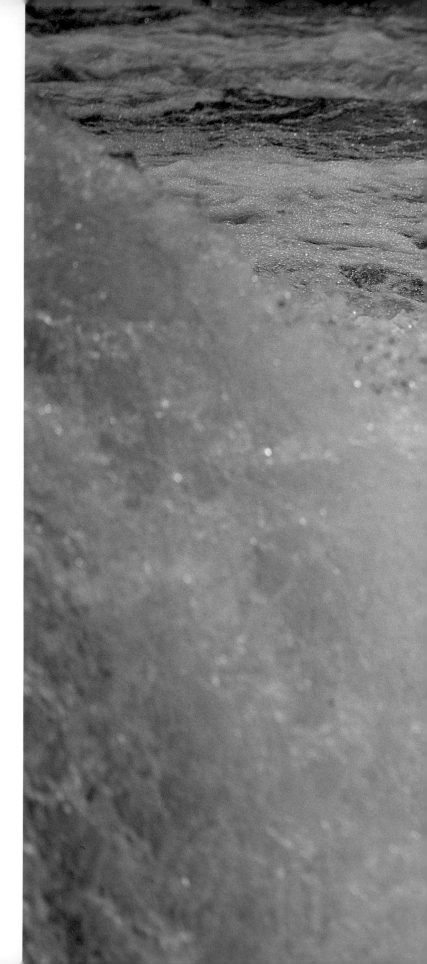

A quiet sunset presides over the calm of Lake Simcoe.
Part of the 386-kilometre Trent–Severn Waterway,
the lake is fed by about eight rivers, and streams.
"The Trent" canal connects Lake Ontario at Trenton to
Lake Huron at Port Severn.

NEAR GAMEBRIDGE BEACH

From Ottawa to Kingston, the Rideau and
Cataraqui rivers along with several lakes, make up
the 202 kilometres of the Rideau Canal system
with 45 locks regulating the route.

RIDEAU LAKES

The six-metre-high Prescott Heritage Harbour Light marks the end of the breakwater sheltering the Prescott marina. It is maintained by the Canadian Coast Guard.

PRESCOTT

A costumed "farmer's wife" in Upper Canada Village demonstrates gardening techniques from the 1860s.

MORRISBURG

Ontario is home to more than 200 different wineries in Niagara, Prince Edward County, the Lake Erie north shore and other emerging regions. According to Jeff Leal, Ontario Minister of Agriculture, Food and Rural Affairs, "Ontario has grown to become Canada's largest wine region — providing more than 7000 direct jobs."

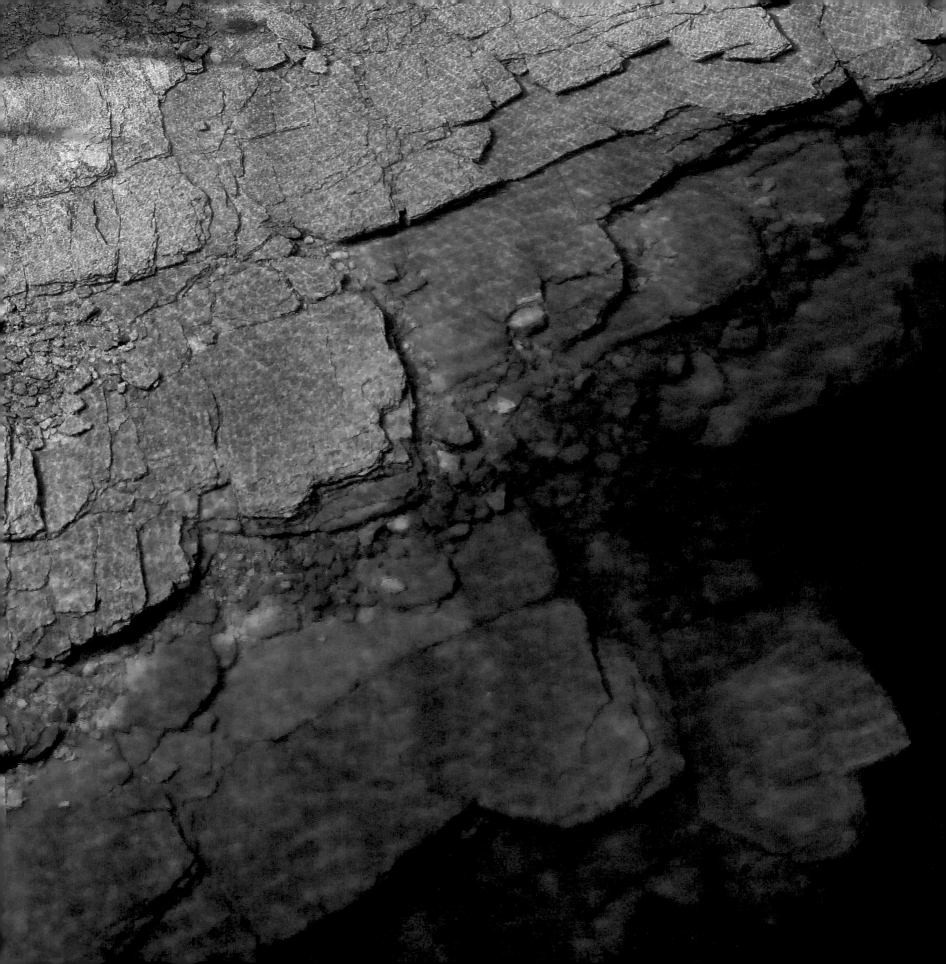

Like the relief on a topographic map, rock layers form on underwater cliffs.

GEORGIAN BAY

Walls of the gorge surround Chedoke Falls where it pours into a turquoise plunge pool. After a rainstorm or snow melt, the pool and river runoffs temporarily turn brown.

HAMILTON

If your feet are travelling the same path, look up for a new perspective. Inspiration is all around.

—George Fischer

The day pushes the last rays of sun through friendly clouds in the southeastern part of Georgina.

UDORA

—244—

Tobermory offers outdoor
enthusiasts countless entertaining
activities, from cliffs and caves to
crystal-clear water. Fathom Five
National Marine Park has preserved
more than 20 historic shipwrecks
that thrill divers and snorkelers.

TOBERMORY

Autumn sunshine seemingly sets a maple forest canopy on fire. Ten of the roughly 150 species of maple are native to Canada.

The tallest of three falls in the Agawa
Canyon, Black Beaver Falls drops
50 metres and runs into the Agawa
River. It is accessible only by the Algoma
Central Railway that travels between
Sault Ste. Marie and Hearst.

ALGOMA

Plunging 22 metres in a free fall, the curtain of water at DeCew Falls provides visitors with a unique view from behind the water. You can get an overview of the falls from the Morningstar Mill during operating hours.

POWER GLEN

George Fischer is one of Canada's most renowned and prolific landscape photographers. He has produced over 50 books, 50 art posters and numerous prints. George's work has appeared on the covers of countless international magazines and newspapers, and in the promotional publications of tourism agencies around the world. Two of his recent publications, *Canada in Colour/en couleurs* and *Exotic Places & Faces*, are stunning compilations of his extensive travels. George's book *Unforgettable Canada* was on *The Globe and Mail*'s bestseller list for eight weeks and sold over 50,000 copies. Other titles in the Unforgettable series include: *Unforgettable Tuscany & Florence, Unforgettable Paris Inoubliable, Unforgettable Atlantic Canada, The 1000 Islands – Unforgettable*, and *Les Îles de la Madeleine Inoubliables*. Currently George is working on a few new books including the *Faroe Islands* and *Canada – 150 Panoramas*. He resides in Toronto, Canada.

See more of George Fischer's work at georgefischerphotography.com

Born in Sablé-sur-Sarthe, France, **Jean-Louis Lepage** traveled extensively across Europe between the ages of 18 and 25. He came to Canada in 1966, settling first in Montréal for 18 months, then moving to Toronto. Jean-Louis has visited at least one different country every year for the past 25 years, and has seen more than 85 countries so far. Since 1991, he has worked as George Fischer's assistant on more than 40 photography books featuring various countries. He likes to travel to the mountainous regions of Mexico in the winter and Europe in the fall. His home base is Toronto, Canada.

ACKNOWLEDGMENTS

I would like to extend my gratitude to Verdiroc/Greenwin for their support, as well as Hanita Braun, Jessica Green and Patricia Castro for all their assistance.

For the "above and beyond" aerial experiences, many thanks to Andy Plater at Owen Sound Flight Services, Keith Saulnier at Georgian Bay Airways, Krishna Patel at the Windsor Flying Club, and Ken Saumure for his awesome heli-skills.

To Jean Lepage who assists me and shares my adventures: I couldn't do it without you.

For pulling it all together and making it look good, I am sincerely thankful for the creativity of Catharine Barker, art director – and E. Lisa Moses, writer and copy editor.

Photo Credits: Sean Fischer, page 64; Ryan Fischer, pages 48, 65

Thank you all!
George Fischer

Cross-country ski trail
NEAR PORT BOLSTER

JEAN-LOUIS LEPAGE

GEORGE FISCHER

Our Moments

The roots of Verdiroc Development Corporation and Greenwin Inc. stretch back to the late 1940s, when the Greenwin Construction Company was first founded by Lipa Green and Arthur Weinstock to build single-family homes in Toronto.

In the early 1950s, Greenwin began residential development in Don Mills, one of Toronto's first suburban satellite communities. From there, we began building multi-unit residential properties. In the 60s and 70s, we constructed more than 10,000 residential units, including single-family homes, condominiums, rental apartment complexes and affordable housing.

Since Verdiroc's inception in 1978 by the late Harold Green, we have transformed Toronto's skyline through our involvement in a wide range of projects, including some of the city's most iconic properties, such as midtown's Castle Hill townhomes, The Ports condominiums at Yonge and St. Clair, and Queen's Park Place in the Bay Street corridor.

With our Hospital Consulting Division, Verdiroc has been instrumental in the redevelopment and enhancement of many of Toronto's leading hospitals. These include Mount Sinai Hospital, Scarborough Hospital, Princess Margaret, Wellesley Hospital, and North York General Hospital.

Building affordable rental housing and giving back to the community have long been the cornerstones of our corporate philosophy. Since 1979, Verdiroc has built upwards of 2,000 affordable rental homes and apartments for a range of clients as well as our own diverse portfolio. Managed by sister company Greenwin Inc., one of Canada's largest privately owned multi-unit residential property

THE HAROLD GREEN BUILDING
121 PARKWAY FOREST DRIVE, TORONTO

management firms, our suites range from market price to affordable rentals, social and non-profit housing.

Headquartered in Toronto, Verdiroc and Greenwin have a combined staff of 500-plus employees. Both brands are featured proudly and prominently throughout central Canada's residential housing landscape. Together, we continue to change the face of urban Canada, operating on a time-tested foundation of innovation, integrity and hands-on involvement that's rooted in an enduring family heritage.

verdiroc.com

greenwin.ca

A crackling campfire pushes back the night chill and the mosquitoes. A perfect Ontario cottage moment.

—George Fischer